HOW TO BE A
SILVER
SURFER

a beginner's guide to the internet

**THIRD
EDITION**
★★★

EMMA ALDRIDGE

The publisher would like to thank Jackie Sherman and Kathy Clarke for their comments on the material contained in this book.

First published in 2001

Second revised edition published in 2003

This third revised edition published in 2006 by Age Concern Books
1268 London Road, London, SW16 4ER, United Kingdom

ISBN-10: 0 86242 421 6
ISBN-13: 978 0 86242 421 3

A catalogue record for this book is available from the British Library.

Edited by Ro Lyon
Page and cover design by Nigel Soper
Typeset by GreenGate Publishing Services, Tonbridge, Kent
Printed and bound in Great Britain by Bell & Bain Ltd, Glasgow

About the author

Emma Aldridge works at Age Concern England. She has played a key part in the organisation's goal of making computer technology and training available more widely to older people, as well as working on a number of other projects. Emma lives in south London with her family.

Photographer: Daniel Sprawson

Acknowledgements

I developed this book from a booklet and CD-ROM, called *Grasp the Nettle: A Beginner's Guide to the Internet*, also published by Age Concern.

The screen examples shown in this book have been generated using *Internet Explorer 6* on a PC. The descriptions apply to *Internet Explorer 5* and above, running on a PC with Windows XP.

Every effort has been made to ensure the content is accurate at the time of writing.

My thanks to all the companies and other organisations for their permission to reproduce screen images taken from their websites.

My thanks to Mum and Dad for putting these chapters to the test, and to Gideon.

Emma Aldridge

Contents

Introduction

Are you one of the many people who wish they could find out more about a favourite radio or television programme after it has ended? Have you been given an email address but not known what to do with it, or wondered about the meaning of this strange language that seems to consist of lots of 'dots', 'ats' and 'coms'?

If you'd like to learn more about the internet and this fantastic way of communicating, fact-finding and sharing information, then this book is for you. Although it will assume that you are not using a computer for the first time, it will still attempt to break through the technical hype and take you on a step-by-step voyage of discovery. It will guide you through what you need to know about how to email and use the web. It will also introduce you to some of the ways in which the internet can help you shop, manage your money, research your family history and chat to people.

All the words that you see in **_bold italics_** are described in the glossary at the end of the book, and many of the websites mentioned are accompanied by screen images of the sites themselves. There is also an index to help you find your way round the book.

What is the internet?

The word '*internet*' is now used so freely in conversation, in news stories and in adverts, for example, that it can be a bit bewildering if you do not understand what it means. In addition there are so many terms which are used interchangeably to describe very similar ideas ('web', 'world wide web', 'net', 'cyberspace', 'information superhighway') that it is no wonder many of us feel confused by the whole thing.

Let's start at the beginning, and since we are talking about communication and information that means starting with a computer.

Some computers are simply stand-alone pieces of equipment. They work in isolation, getting on with the jobs that are required of them but they do not meet or talk to anyone else.

Other computers are more sociable. They are connected to each other, and like members of a large community, they can share things with each other. This sort of computer community is called a **network**.

The internet is simply a global network of computers all linked to each other through communication connections such as telephone lines. When you use one of these computers to access the internet you are '*online*'.

> Other types of equipment can also be connected in order to share information and communicate with each other, such as digital television sets, mobile telephones and video-game consoles. In this book, however, we concentrate on how you can use a computer to get started on the internet.

Getting and sharing information

Every computer connected to the internet is owned or used by people and organisations with information and expertise to share on just about any topic you can imagine. Being a member of the internet 'club' is therefore like being a member of an enormous global library. The internet equivalent to shelves crammed with millions of books and journals is the world wide web (www) or the **web** for short.

Instead of reading the pages of a book, you simply look at the relevant pages of a **website** (sometimes referred to as 'surfing the web'). It can also be a lot more exciting because you don't just have words, but can look at pictures and moving images, sometimes accompanied by sound, and you normally get the chance to communicate with the 'authors' of the website.

Communicating

Something else you can do when you get access to the internet is send messages almost instantaneously to friends, family and other people all over the world. You do this by using **email**, short for electronic mail, which is the internet's version of the postal service. Instead of putting a letter into the postbox and having to wait days for it to be picked up, delivered and a reply to arrive, you simply type a message on the computer keyboard, address it using an **email address**, and at the press of a key on your keyboard send it immediately to another computer anywhere in the world.

Meeting people

The most popular aspect of the internet is that it is interactive. Not only can you find information about anything and everything at any time of the day, but if you want to, you can also chat to other people looking for the same sort of things.

Email is a great way to swap messages with a person or a chosen group of people, but you can also use the internet to share opinions, ideas and gossip with groups of new people all at once, by joining a **message board, chat site,** or **mailing list**.

What else?

If that's not enough for you, the internet can also provide you with new ways to:

* research and book holidays, travel and other leisure-time activities;
* read the latest news from any part of the world;
* listen to repeats of radio programmes;
* play your favourite game or bet against opponents who may be sitting at their computers on the other side of the world;
* shop for books, food, presents and clothing; and
* manage your personal finances.

Once you have access to the internet, the whole world is at your fingertips.

How do I get connected?

The good news is that you do not need to have the latest or the most expensive computer. A computer bought new a few years ago that you currently use for word processing or that you've been given second-hand, for example, can be used to get you onto the internet – it just might be a bit slower.

Minimum requirements for connecting to the internet

To connect your computer to the internet you will need the following:

A Pentium® 233MHz processor, as minimum
One of the key factors in determining how quickly your computer will work is its *processor* speed. The faster the processor (measured in MHz, which stands for megahertz, or gigahertz (GHz) which are faster than megahertz), the more calculations and data the computer can process. A computer with a 233MHz processor is sufficient for the internet. The most common type of processor is called a 'Pentium®'. If you hope to do lots of work with photos, sounds or video clips, it is advisable to check that your computer has at least a 700MHz processor.

At least 150MB free on your hard disk
The disk inside your computer that stores *software* and data is called the 'hard disk'. The amount of disk space a computer has is measured in megabytes (MB), or gigabytes (GB) which are larger than megabytes.

A second-hand computer with a relatively small hard disk capacity of 480MB, for example, will not prevent you getting onto the internet – it simply means that your computer will hold a lot less information and fewer software programs than a newer computer with a hard disk capacity of

500GB. However, your computer will need at least 150MB of unused disk space to hold the software required to connect to the internet and the data you will accumulate.

> If you are unsure how much free disk space is available on your computer's hard disk, a simple way to check is to go to the 'Start' menu, select 'My Computer', select 'Local Disk (C:)' and on the left-hand side beneath the label 'Details' you will see the amount of free space listed.

At least 64MB RAM

RAM stands for *Random Access Memory*. It temporarily stores and accesses information on your computer. A computer with at least 64MB of RAM (but preferably more) will be sufficient to access the internet.

> If you are unsure about the type of processor or the amount of RAM you have in your computer, a simple way to check is to go to 'My Computer' and on the left-hand side select the link labelled 'View System Information'.

A CD-ROM drive

Computer CDs are identical in appearance to music CDs. They are a convenient way of storing a lot of data. A CD that can only be read from is called a CD-ROM (ROM stands for 'Read Only Memory') and a CD which can be saved to is called a CD-RW (RW stands for 'Rewritable').

A CD-ROM drive provides a simple way for you to load the software required to connect to the internet onto your computer.

A modem or router

A *modem* is a device that either fits inside your computer (an internal modem) or is a box which is linked via a cable to your computer (an external modem). It allows your computer to communicate with other computers over a standard telephone line. The most common ways to access the internet are via a *dial-up* account or by using *broadband* (see the section 'Broadband versus dial-up' further on in this chapter for a more detailed description of the difference between the two). These two methods of connection each require a different type of modem.

Dial-up modem

All new computers come with an internal dial-up modem fitted as standard. Not all second-hand computers will be supplied with modems, though, so you may need to buy one separately from a computer store, by mail order or through a computer magazine at a cost of about £50. Internal modems are more complicated to install, so you may need to pay a technician to do this for you or choose an external modem instead.

Whether you decide on an internal or external dial-up modem, check that the modem is 56K and V.92 standard. This means that it will transfer information such as web pages and email messages at a speed of 56 kilobits per second (Kbps) to/from your computer, which is the fastest speed possible over a standard telephone line. The 'V.92' means that it will offer features such as a quicker connection time.

ADSL modem

If you are interested in faster broadband internet access, the most common way of connecting is via an **ADSL** modem. ADSL stands for Asymmetric Digital Subscriber Line; the term 'asymmetric' refers to the fact that data moves faster from the telephone exchange to a home computer than in the other direction. This makes it particularly suitable for internet use, where more information is received than is sent.

Many **Internet Service Providers** will provide you with a basic ADSL modem. But if you prefer to purchase your own, they are widely available and cost upwards of £50.

If you want more than one computer to share the internet connection, then choose a **router** (which will have an in-built modem). If you want to avoid having cables trailing over floors and round doorways, or you have a laptop computer, then a convenient solution is to opt for a wireless router. Routers cost upwards of £65, and like modems are widely available from computer stores, by mail order, through a computer magazine or online.

A spare USB port

A **USB port** is a type of connection socket found on the front or back of your computer. Cables from **hardware** devices such as printers, scanners, modems, routers and digital cameras slot into this type of socket and data from your computer can quickly be shared with them.

A telephone line

Your computer connects to other computers on the internet via your telephone line. Sounds simple, doesn't it? Well it is ... but a little planning will help you avoid some possible pitfalls.

You can use your existing telephone line for internet use, but if you are using a modem you will need a way of switching between the computer and your voice telephone. For a couple of pounds you can buy a useful little accessory called a microfilter (also known as a 'splitter' or 'socket doubler') from electrical retailers – it allows you to keep both your computer and your telephone connected to the telephone socket at the same time.

A disadvantage of sharing a single telephone line between a modem and your telephone, is that you cannot make or receive telephone (voice) calls while connected to the internet. If you access the internet a lot, this might get a bit frustrating for friends and family who try to ring you. It also presents a problem should you need to call an internet helpline as you won't be able to talk and be online (to describe the problem you're having) at the same time, unless you use a mobile phone. If you find this a nuisance you could install an additional telephone line. Your telephone operator will give you a new telephone number for the line, and you will be able to choose the room in which you want the socket installed. The cost of an additional telephone line varies between different telephone operators, but expect to pay around £50 for the connection and around £10 each month for the rental.

A good all-round solution is to install broadband as it allows you to make and receive telephone calls while you are accessing the internet, without requiring a separate telephone line. There are a few limitations to its use, however, and additional costs, all of which are discussed in the section on broadband further on in this chapter.

If you have cable television or cable telephone, or live in an area where cable services are available, then you may be able to get a fast internet connection by cable. The monthly charge for this service may work out to be more expensive than the rental of a standard telephone line, and in a few cases you have to purchase a special cable modem, but the monthly charge is likely to cover all your internet access, no matter how long you spend online.

Anti-virus software and firewall

A computer connected to the internet is at risk from dangerous files called *viruses* that move between computers. You should get, or check that your computer has been installed with, anti-virus software and *firewall* software that allows only specific kinds of messages from the internet to flow in and out. Both types of software will automatically perform regular updates, and will periodically advise you of software upgrades that you can buy to help protect against the latest threats to your computer. You can download free copies of anti-virus software and firewall software, often for trial periods (such as Grisoft's *AVG* for example); or you can buy the software (such as Symantec's *Norton* or *McAfee,* which cost about £40 to £50), which gives you regular and more comprehensive updates, as well as support should you require it.

A router will give your computer added security from viruses as routers contain a built-in firewall.

Broadband versus dial-up

Think about how you like to read an engrossing novel. Isn't it more satisfying to have an unlimited amount of time to read at leisure, instead of dipping in and out and reading it in short snippets? Broadband gives you this sort of freedom with the internet. It gives you an 'always on' connection, which means that your computer maintains a permanent connection to the internet. The alternative is dial-up, which means creating a temporary connection to the Internet every time you go online.

Broadband also has the advantage of enabling computers to transfer data at high speeds, which not only means that you have a faster connection, but that you can also send (known as *uploading*) and receive (known as *downloading*) large amounts of information over the internet, such as photographs, music and video broadcasts, for example, that dial-up would struggle with.

Broadband does make you more vulnerable to viruses than with dial-up, especially as you are more likely to leave your computer switched on, so do ensure that anti-virus and firewall software are installed on your computer and that you keep them up to date.

If you plan to be a very light, occasional user of the internet, then broadband will probably work out more expensive than dial-up, although prices are tumbling all the time. In some rural areas broadband is not available.

Choosing an Internet Service Provider

An **Internet Service Provider** (ISP) provides you with the means to send and receive information over the telephone line to and from your computer. Think of them as being like a telephone exchange. Your modem dials a special telephone number supplied by the ISP which calls one of the ISP's modems. This connects you to the rest of the internet for the time that you are connected to your ISP.

If you buy a new computer you are usually invited to sign up with a particular ISP, which can make things easy, but you might find that you can get a better deal by doing a little research first.

One way to get online for the first time is to pick up a CD which allows you to sign up with an ISP. You can find them in shops or supermarkets or attached to the pages of computer magazines. You then simply put the CD into the drive on your computer and follow the instructions given to you on the screen. Once online you can switch to another ISP by visiting their website.

Examples of ISPs you may have heard of are: BT, NTL, AOL, Wanadoo, Tiscali and Claranet. The number of ISPs, and the packages they each offer, is bewildering, so shopping around can be a complicated business. The main options offered by most ISPs are:

Pay-as-you-go dial-up – you access the internet using a standard telephone line. You are charged according to the amount of time you spend on the internet, at the rate of making a local telephone call, so half an hour's connection on a BT line would cost you about 30 pence off-peak or £1.13 peak. If you think you will only use the internet for email and occasional web use (fewer than about 15 hours a month), then this will probably be your best option.

Subscription dial-up – you access the internet using a standard telephone line and pay a flat monthly fee. Read the terms and conditions carefully. Almost all require a BT line. Some packages only allow unlimited use between certain times. Most set limits on your time online (for example 120 or 150 hours over the course of a month). Packages giving you unlimited use any time of the day are often referred to as 'AnyTime' packages, and typically cost around £15 a month.

Broadband – most broadband packages charge a monthly fee but limit how much information you can download and upload each month (known as your **bandwidth**), and you pay if you exceed this limit. Many ISPs offer only annual contracts, so you are tied to them for a year, but include a free ADSL modem and free setup. Others offer more flexible monthly contracts but require you to reimburse them if you terminate the contract after a short period, or they charge you for the modem.

Common questions about choosing an ISP
'How reliable is the ISP going to be?'
This is difficult to determine. The major ISPs have massive connections to the internet which means that they can support a very large number of simultaneous users without grinding to a halt. However, big is not always best. If they over-subscribe then bottlenecks can occur, resulting in difficulties dialling-in and slower connections during busy periods. Computer magazines and consumer guides, such as *Which?,* publish guides to help you compare the reliability and performance of different ISPs. Back up your research by talking to friends and relatives already on the internet – either they will sing the praises of their ISP or recount their frustrations, giving you a fairly good idea of how they fare.

'What support is available and what are the costs?'
Some ISPs only provide support online, so it will not be personalised or step-by-step support. Those that offer 24-hour telephone support may charge calls at the national rate, or at a premium call rate of 50p or more per minute.

'Can you add multiple email accounts? What kind of email addresses are you given?'
Almost all ISPs now allow you to set up more than one email account. So, for example, two people using one computer can each have a personalised

email address and access to their own email messages. They also offer web-based email (usually shortened to '**webmail**') as standard, so that you can access your messages from any computer connected to the internet. Even better are ISPs which allow you something called a **POP3** email address rather than a webmail address. POP3 allows you to use popular email applications, such as *Outlook* or *Outlook Express*, to read and write emails without having to be online all the time. This saves you money on your telephone bill.

'Does the ISP provide space for your own web page? How much space?'

You rarely pay a premium for web space and most ISPs offer it, so the chances are that it will be bundled with whatever internet package you choose whether you decide to use it or not. The amount of space offered varies between ISPs – 10MB is at the lower end and will be sufficient for displaying a range of your favourite photographs. If you plan to build a website incorporating a lot of audio, video or photographs, then you might need more. However, web space is cheap to buy at a later stage, so it should be the least influential factor in choosing between ISPs and internet packages.

'Is it easy to change ISPs?'

With so many internet packages and offers available, it is not unusual to switch from one ISP to another. But check the small print for cancellation fees, minimum 12-month contracts, equipment leases and notice periods. If you want to give yourself the option of switching easily from one broadband provider to another, then check that the ISP will give you what is called a 'MAC code', which lets you switch without losing a broadband connection. Email can cause the most disruption. If the name of your ISP is included in your email address then check that your old ISP will allow you to continue to receive emails to your old address for a limited period, to give you time to notify everyone of your change of email address.

Going wireless

Just like mobiles and cordless handsets have changed the way we use the telephone, connecting computers without wires to a telephone line opens up new possibilities for using the internet.

Getting a wireless internet connection for a laptop will allow you to enjoy the freedom of being able to access the internet from anywhere in the home. Sharing a wireless broadband connection between two or more computers will cut down on unsightly (and potentially hazardous) spaghetti wiring.

You will need one wireless router, and a 'wireless adapter' for each of the computers you want to be able to communicate with this router. Many new laptops will come with a wireless adapter built in; otherwise you simply buy a card that slots in. Desktop computers can be upgraded by fitting a wireless adapter into a spare USB port. Adapters cost about £30 each and can be bought online or are widely available in shops selling computer equipment.

4

How do I use the web?

Getting started

Just like a library of books and journals, the world wide web, or web for short, enables access to sources of information, called websites.

To load and display pages in a website you will need a piece of software called a **web browser**. Currently the most popular web browser is *Internet Explorer* which is included as part of the Microsoft Windows **operating system.** You will find it on your desktop (see Fig 1) or by going to the 'Start' menu, selecting 'Programs' then 'Internet Explorer'.

If you cannot find a web browser on your computer, then this free piece of software can be found on the CDs provided by ISPs.

Fig 1 – You can open *Internet Explorer* from your desktop

New improved versions of these browsers, with new features, are released from time to time. It is best to use the most recent version of a browser, provided that your computer has sufficient memory and speed to support it.

The back, forward, stop, refresh, home, search, favourites, print, address bar and history functions of *Internet Explorer* (see Fig 2) are common to most browsers, although the wording and location of menu options and buttons might differ. The main functions are:

Back & Forward – allow you to retrace your steps and move to pages recently visited.

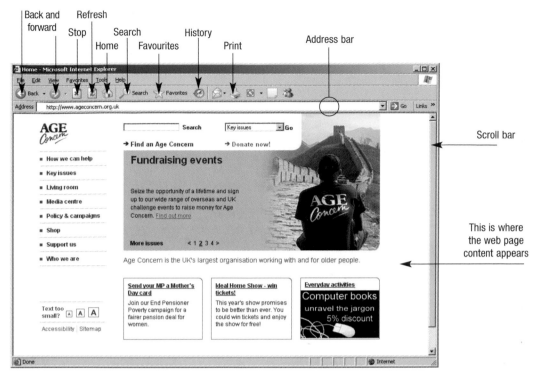

Fig 2 – A typical web page showing the main features of *Internet Explorer*

Stop – allows you to stop loading a page if you clicked on a **hyperlink** with your mouse by accident or if a page is taking too long to appear.

Refresh – updates any web page stored temporarily on the hard disk of your computer with the latest copy of that web page. This is useful when you return to a page that you've visited recently because your browser will automatically display the page that is stored in the temporary area on your computer's hard disk (the **cache**), rather than the current page on the web which may have changed in the meantime.

Home – takes you to the page that appears when you first connect to the internet.

Search – displays a quick link to a **search engine** called 'MSN search' in the left of your browser screen, providing one way to search the web (see the section 'Searching the web' further on in this chapter for other ways).

Favourites – links to websites that you can save for easy reference later on.

History – gives you a list of the websites you have recently visited.

Print – allows you to print the current web page if your computer is connected to a printer.

The **address bar** – displays the address of the current web page.

The **scroll bar** – click on the scroll bar with your mouse to move up and down a web page.

Reading pages on the web is different from reading pages in a book. Rather than having a single route from one page to the next, you move around a website, and between websites, by clicking your mouse on <u>underlined text</u> and graphics (**hyperlinks)** which link to other pages.

You can always spot where the hyperlinks are on a web page because the text is usually underlined or displayed in a different colour to the rest of the text. Also, as you move your mouse over a hyperlink, the pointer changes shape to look more like a pointing hand 🖑 and the title of the destination page is often displayed in the bottom left of your browser (see Fig 3).

The words 'Weather Home' act as a hyperlink

This is the web address of the page the hyperlink will take you to

Fig 3 – The BBC website (*bbc.co.uk*). As the mouse rolls over the words 'Weather Home' the arrow head changes to a hand (not shown), and a message appears in the bottom left-hand corner of the screen indicating the hyperlink's destination page

Common questions

'What happens if I turn off my computer while I am still connected to the internet?'

There is no need to worry. If you are using broadband, it is designed to be 'always on'; you don't pay by the minute. If you are on a 'pay-as-you-go' package, you won't be running up a huge telephone bill either just because you forgot to select 'disconnect' before switching off your computer. Closing down your computer automatically disconnects you from the internet.

'The text is too small for me to read properly – can I make it bigger?'

You only need to make a couple of simple changes in your browser settings to increase or decrease the size of text to make it easier to read. Some websites, though, are designed in such a way that the text size is locked and cannot be adjusted.

In *Internet Explorer,* select 'View' from the very top of your browser window and select 'Text Size'. A drop-down menu will appear. From this, select 'largest' through to 'smallest' to increase/decrease the size of the text.

You may find that changing the font size distorts graphic and text alignments in some pages, in which case you can always change the text size again until you are satisfied with the balance between readability and page layout.

'I have trouble with some colours – can I control the colour settings of web pages myself?'

You can make a simple change to your web browser to change the colour settings to make web pages easier to read. But as with text size, some websites are designed in such a way that your web browser will not be able to override its colour settings.

To change colour settings using *Internet Explorer,* select the 'Tools' menu, then select 'Internet Options' and then from the 'General' option select 'Colors'.

'Why do I sometimes have to wait a long time for pictures on web pages to appear?'

Web pages can consist of many individual elements – menu bars, logos, advertisements, photographs, etc – which load one at a time and build up a web page like a jigsaw. If your connection to the internet slows down, which often happens at peak times when many other people are attempting to connect to the internet through the same ISP or connect to the same page as you, then these web page elements will take much longer to load and display on your computer.

'Can I change the page that appears first when I connect to the internet?'

Yes, this is very useful when you find a website you know you will want to come back to time and time again. Go to the page that you want to appear when you first connect to the internet to check the web address. In *Internet Explorer,* select the 'Tools' menu, then select 'Internet Options', then ensure the 'General' option is selected. Click on the button labelled 'Use Current' (see Fig 4) and the address of your page will be inserted. Select 'Apply' to save it. Now when you click on the 'Home' button on your browser, this page will automatically load.

Fig 4 – Select a web address to be your new home page;
for example *The Telegraph*

Searching the web

Many people find that it is fun to explore the web by surfing from site to site, going wherever the hyperlinks take them. But when you are trying to find something specific, and find it as soon as possible, you will need to go through a process of searching for the information you are after, and on the web you have two different ways. You can either search directly by address or by using the equivalent of a telephone directory.

Web addresses

If you look carefully at the posters on a bus, the adverts in a newspaper, or the next letter from your bank, the chances are that you will find a reference somewhere to a **web address** as a way of finding out more information. For many businesses, a web address is as important as a telephone or fax number.

These web addresses – or *Uniform Resource Locators (URLs)*, which is their more technical but far less descriptive name – look complex and must be typed in with care so as not to make any typing errors or leave any characters out.

To visit a website via its web address, you simply type the address into the address bar and press the 'Return' key on your keyboard.

If you understand the components of a web address it can help you understand more about the site you visit. web addresses typically look something like this:

http://www.bbc.co.uk

http://www – this part tells your web browser that it is looking for a website. The 'www' literally stands for 'world wide web'. However, web browsers have become more sophisticated and now tend to allow you to 'drop' the 'http://www' so that you only need to type **bbc.co.uk**

bbc – this is the name of the website itself.

.co - this part describes the kind of website it is. **.co** indicates a company. Other common ones you may encounter are **.org** to indicate a not-for-profit organisation and **.gov** to indicate government. The 'dot' itself is very important and is typed in using the full-stop character on your keyboard.

.uk – this part describes the country of origin. Again the 'dot' is important and must not be missed out.

Search engines and directories

If you do not have the right web address to hand, or you just want to conduct a more general search, then you will find search engines and directories invaluable as they provide the internet's equivalent of a telephone directory service.

They are websites in themselves and include a search box on their first page allowing you to enter a word or phrase to describe the topic you are interested in, and some provide a list of subjects and categories that you can choose from.

One of the most popular is 'Google' (google.co.uk). It combs the internet on a regular basis to bring you new websites and updates to websites just like any other search engine, but it also offers a clean, uncluttered website and is very fast. Google also features a button called 'I'm Feeling Lucky' which takes you directly to the website which most closely fits your search request.

Finding a needle in a haystack: tips for better searching

The volume of information available on the web can work against you if you are trying to find something specific and have to wade through pages and pages before you get to one that looks vaguely useful or interesting, so follow these guidelines to reduce the number of false leads:

1. Narrow down your search by geography

Many search tools offer the facility to search the entire web or to limit the search to information with a UK bias. It may be useful to expand your search for general research purposes, but limit your site when you are looking for local information.

2. Watch your spelling!

A lot of the time your search will be fruitless because it has been spelt incorrectly. Luckily, Google has a spellchecker, so if you type in **'cathederal'** for example, it will ask you **'Did you mean cathedral?'**

3. Be persistent and creative

Often on the internet it does not matter whether you use capital or lower-case letters. When you are searching, however, it's best to use capital letters for names of people, places and titles.

If you enter just one keyword into your search, you'll end up with far too many results. You can make searches more specific by typing two or more words. For example, just entering the word **'bridge'** delivers thousands of results, whereas a search on **'bridge card game'** lists a far more specific set of results (see Figs 5 and 6).

Surrounding multiple keywords with speech marks (" ") – or joining them with **AND, +, a comma**, or **&** – can be useful when searching for a phrase, or person or film title.

Fig 5 – A search on the word 'bridge' using *google.co.uk* returns a long list of results

Fig 6 – A more descriptive search phrase such as 'bridge card game' returns more useful results

4. Read the help
The techniques for refining searches vary between search tools. Get to know the one you like best by reading the 'advanced' sections.

Understanding the search results
To view any of the web pages returned from your search, click with your mouse on the page title which usually appears in blue underlined text. The paragraph of text beneath the page title usually gives you a little more information about the contents.

It can help to keep the search results page open, while opening web pages you choose from this page (known as opening a separate window). Click on the page title with the *right* mouse button and a pop-up menu will appear. Revert back to your *left* mouse button and click 'Open link in new window'.

To move between windows, click with your mouse on the one you want from the 'Taskbar' at the bottom of your screen, or hold down the 'Alt' key and tap the 'Tab' key on your keyboard until you reach the window you want, then release.

Opening multiple windows will slow down your computer, so it is good practice to close the additional windows after you have finished with them.

Common questions

'What is meant by a 'dot com?' I hear the term a lot in relation to the internet.'
The term literally means '.com'. The majority of web addresses end with **.com** (short for 'company') – for example **lastminute.com**

'Is there a simple way to revisit a website?'
Surfing the web is like a journey and your web browser will remember your route. At any stage in your journey you can retrace your steps. To move sequentially through the pages you have visited recently, use the 'Back' and 'Forward' buttons in your browser menu. To jump straight to a particular page, click the down-pointing arrow at the end of the address bar with your mouse to select from the list of pages, or click the 'History' button – the pages will be listed in the left-hand pane of your browser screen (see Fig 7).

Selecting the 'History' button gives you a list of the web pages you have previously visited

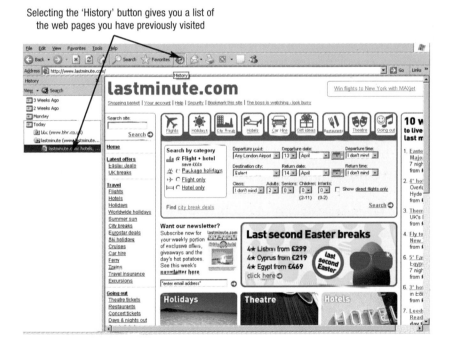

Fig 7 – Retrace your steps by selecting 'History' and then pick a page from the list in the left-hand pane of web pages that you have recently visited

'How can I tell the difference between an advertisement and an unbiased search result?'
A lot of search engines are funded by the money they earn from advertisers, who in turn are keen for you to click on a link to their website intentionally or by mistake.

Look closely again at Fig 6. The results page is divided into separate sections. The results at the top of the page and the results on the right of the page are preceded by the heading 'Sponsored Link(s)', which means that companies have paid for these prominent promotions, and the links tend to take you to pages designed to entice you into buying something, which is not always what you had in mind. With some search tools the give-away is the words 'sponsored result' next to a web address.

Bookmarking favourite websites

Once you have found a page that you like, you can 'bookmark' it for future reference. This means that you never need to remember the route you took to find the page again, or the web address of the page itself; you simply select 'Favourites' from the *Internet Explorer* menu and choose the page you want to revisit.

To add a new website to your list of favourites, select 'Favourites' from the *Internet Explorer* menu, followed by 'Add' or 'Add to Favourites'.

Tips when bookmarking

Edit the text that is used to describe your Favourite. Text contained in the web page will automatically be suggested, but change it if you think it is not very helpful.

If you create a lot of Favourites, it can be useful to organise them into logical categories (called 'folders'). You can decide what these categories should be called – for example you might want to have a set of Favourites organised within a 'travel' category. To create a new folder, select 'Favourites' from the Internet Explorer menu, followed by 'Organize' or 'Organize Favourites', followed by 'Create Folder'. Type over the text labelled 'New Folder' in

---

dark blue with your own category title (such as 'travel') and then select 'Close'.

Tidy up your Favourites once in a while by deleting them, especially if a web page you previously bookmarked no longer exists or is no longer relevant.

If you are using dial-up access to the internet and want to limit the amount of time you spend connected, then you can choose to view a favourite web page *offline*. To do this, connect to the internet, select the 'Favourites' menu, followed by 'Add to Favourites', and then select the box labelled 'Make available offline' to leave a tick ( ). Next time you want to view the page, select it from your Favourites list. Remember that even though you do not need to be online to view this page in future, the links you follow from that page will not be available without going online. To ensure that you are looking at an up-to-date version, select 'Synchronize' from the 'Tools' menu (which briefly opens a connection to the internet, and closes it when completed).

5

How can I send and receive emails?

Email is a cheap way of sending a message to someone – even if you are sending it to Australia, you only pay the cost of a local telephone call and the cost doesn't increase with size (a weighty 100-page document will cost the same as a single line of text).

The information about who an email message is for and how they can be located is all wrapped up within the email address.

When you sign up with an **Internet Service Provider (ISP)** you will be given an email account and will have the opportunity to choose or change your email address. You may have heard an email address given out on a radio or television programme and puzzled over the meaning of the strange-sounding expressions. A typical email address looks something like this:

heatherbloggs@hotmail.com

heatherbloggs is the unique name that you choose for your email address. Sometimes names are separated by a full-stop; for example **heather.bloggs**

@ is pronounced 'at'.

hotmail.com is the name of your ISP or whoever is providing your email address (in this example hotmail), and is pronounced 'hotmail **dot** com'.

Sending an email

1. Start up your email program

The email program that comes with *Internet Explorer* is called *Outlook Express.* You will find it on your desktop; alternatively, you can go to the 'Start' menu, select 'Programs' and then 'Outlook Express'. If you have *Microsoft Office* software installed on your computer (in order to produce word-processed documents like letters, for example) then you will be able to use an alternative email program, called *Outlook,* which can be opened via the desktop or the 'Start' menu.

Email programs, like web browsers, differ slightly from each other but they all perform the same basic functions, as shown in Fig 8.

Inbox – Lists all of the emails you have received.

Outbox – Emails waiting to be sent will be stored here temporarily.

Sent Items – Emails which have been sent are listed here.

Create Mail or **New** – Create a new message.

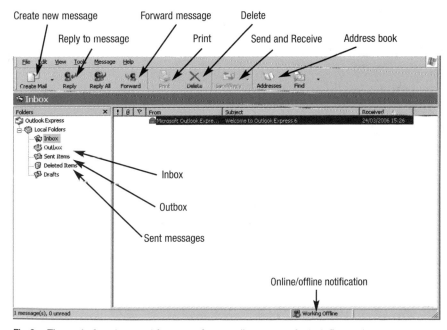

Fig 8 – The main functions and features of an email program *(Outlook Express)*

Reply – Reply to a message that you have received.

Forward – Send the message on to another person.

Delete – Remove the email message (it is not deleted permanently; it is held in the 'Deleted Items' folder until permanently deleted).

Addresses or **Address book** – Add, remove or amend email addresses in your address book.

Send/Recv or **Send/Receive** – Make a connection to the internet to send any email messages in your Outbox and receive any new messages that have been sent to you.

If you are using dial-up access to the internet, your email program may try to connect you to the internet straightaway, but the only time that you actually need to make a connection is when you finally want to send your completed email. So, for the time being, stop the connection being made (for example select 'cancel' or 'work offline'). If you are using broadband you are paying for the privilege of having a permanent online connection to the internet, so you do not need to disconnect.

2. Create a new message

To compose a new message, click on the button labelled 'Create Mail'. (If you are using *Outlook* rather than *Outlook Express* the button is labelled 'New').

3. Enter the email address

In the box labelled 'To:', type in the email address of the person you are sending the email to. If this is someone that you regularly email, you will find the 'address book' facility useful because it allows you to keep a record of the email addresses which you use frequently and then pick them out without retyping them when you are creating a new message (see Fig 9).

You can also send a copy of the message to another person at the same time, by typing in their email address, or adding it from your address book, in the box labelled 'Cc:' (Cc stands for 'Carbon copy').

Click on the name you want,
then click the 'To:' button

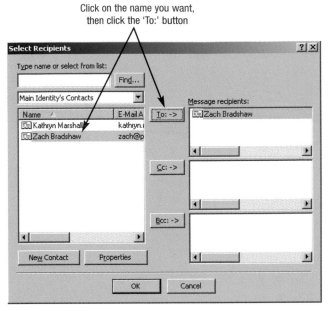

Fig 9 – Use the address book to pick out email addresses which you use frequently

If you want to send a copy of your email to someone else in secret, then type in their email address, or add it from your address book, in the box labelled 'Bcc:' (short for 'Blind carbon copy'). That person will receive the message, but their email address will not be listed, so the other person or people it has been sent to will be unaware of this additional recipient.

4. Type in the subject of your email
In the box labelled 'Subject:', type in a single word or short phrase to describe your message. This subject will appear in the recipient's email Inbox.

5. Write your message
Your message can be as long or as short as you like, and as formal or informal as you want to be. It is a good habit to check over your spelling before you send your message by clicking on the 'Spelling' button or selecting 'Spelling' from the 'Tools' menu.

You can also send ('attach') files from your computer together with your text message. This is ideal for sending something like a scanned photograph or a more detailed letter or report electronically.

Simply click on the button labelled 'Attach' (sometimes pictured as a paperclip 📎) or select 'File Attachment' from the 'Insert' menu, then browse through the files and folders on your computer, select the file you want to attach, then select 'Attach' or 'Insert'.

Fig 10 – Writing an email using *Outlook Express*

6. Send your message

You can send your message as soon as you finish writing it by clicking on the button labelled 'Send'. If you are using dial-up access to the internet this will open a connection with your ISP.

If you are using dial-up, you can save money by saving your message(s) by selecting 'File' followed by 'Send Later' – they will be kept in your Outbox until you are ready to go online and then all be sent at once. Sending 20 messages like this will cost about the same as sending one!

How does it work?

When you make a connection to your ISP and send an email, your message is sent down the telephone line to a huge computer managed by your ISP called a *mail server*. At this point you can disconnect from your ISP if you are using dial-up. The ISP's mail server then sends the message to its final destination, which is coded within the email address.

If you are using dial-up and want to ensure that you are working offline when *Outlook Express* opens (and therefore choose for yourself when you wish to make a connection to your ISP to go online), go to the *Outlook Express* 'Tools' menu, select 'Options' and go to the 'General' tab. Ensure that the 'Send and receive messages at startup' box does *not* have a tick ☐ in it.

Receiving an email

Receiving and responding to an email is much simpler. Click on the button labelled 'Send/Recv' in *Outlook Express* ('Send/Receive' in *Outlook).* Any new email messages that have been sent to you will appear in your Inbox.

To read a message, open up your Inbox and double-click on the message you want to open.

If you want to reply, click on the button labelled 'Reply'. A new message box will be opened which automatically contains the email address of the person who has sent you the message and contains the same subject name preceded with the letters 'Re:' to indicate that it is a reply. Enter your message, and then send your reply.

If you want to send the message onto another person, click on the button labelled 'Forward'. A new message box will be opened with space for you to specify the email address of the person you want to forward the message to, space for you to add your own comment or note, and the same subject name preceded with the letters 'Fw:' to indicate that it is a forwarded message. Be aware, however, that if the original message was a large file it could result in an unnecessarily long internet connection, so remember to delete any unnecessary text/attachments that you do not want to forward with your comment or note.

When you open your Inbox you will be able to spot at a glance any emails that have been sent with an attached file. The Attachments symbol (📎) will appear next to the message. With the message open, you can double-click on the attachment to open it. You can also save the attachment to a folder on your own computer by selecting 'Save Attachments' from the 'File' menu.

Emails will be stored in your Inbox until you choose to move or delete them.

As you build up an assorted collection of email messages, you may find it helpful to organise your messages into folders. To create a new folder, select the 'File' menu, followed by 'Folder', followed by 'New' and type in a name for the new folder. You can then highlight any of the messages currently in your Inbox and drag them into this new folder.

How does it work?

When someone sends an email message to you, it is stored on your ISP's mail server until you request it. When you are connected to your ISP, the message is sent down your telephone line to your computer via your modem and is stored in your email Inbox.

Common questions

'I access the internet using dial-up. How can I minimise the amount of time I spend online when using email?'
You do not need to be online to read or write an email – only when you want to send or receive a message. So when you receive an email, disconnect from your ISP and read your message at leisure. You can even set *Outlook Express* to automatically disconnect from your ISP immediately after it has completed the Send and Receive, so you don't have to remember to do it yourself. From the 'Tools' menu, select 'Options' and click on the 'Connection' tab. Ensure that the 'Hang-up after sending and receiving' box has a tick (☑) in it.

'Will I still be able to receive emails even if I switch off my computer?'
Yes. An email isn't actually transmitted directly to your computer: instead it is held by your ISP in space that they 'reserve' on their mail server for your email messages – it's just like having your own pigeon-hole. It is only when you are connected to your ISP that any emails in your 'pigeon-hole' are actually downloaded to your Inbox.

'Can I send and receive emails on any computer?'
Yes, but you will need to set up a webmail account such as a 'hotmail' account (so-called because your email address will take the form **yourname@hotmail.com**). To set up a 'hotmail' account, go to the

website **hotmail.com** With a webmail account you can go to any computer connected to the internet (for example, imagine going on holiday and visiting an internet café), visit the same website, enter your username and password and send/receive emails using that account. These email accounts are free but while you are writing your message or reading your emails you are online, so with a dial-up connection you are paying for every minute.

'My friend has sent me an email with an attachment but when I open up the attached document it is completely unreadable. Why is this?'
Don't worry – you are not doing anything wrong. This happens when someone sends you a document which has been created using software that you are not running on your own computer, or a different *version* of the software to the one you are using. As a result your computer cannot interpret the document and either cannot open the document at all or, in trying to interpret it, scrambles the contents. The best thing to do is to contact your friend, resolve whether they are trying to send you a document that you simply will not be able to open because you do not have the right piece of software, or whether you do have the software but will need the file to be saved as a different version and then be sent again.

'How do I know that my email has been sent successfully?'
To check that a message has left your computer, open up your 'Sent' folder. The message should appear in the list (at the top of the list if it is sorted by date).

If your email was not correctly addressed – for example you misspelled the person's name or typed a comma by mistake into the email address – then you will be sent a failure message to inform you that the email was not delivered. If the mistake is obvious, correct it and send the email again. If you are writing an email and are unsure whether you have a correct email address, you could end your message by asking the person to reply back to you to acknowledge that they have received it. Allow them a little bit of time to reply, and if they don't, then try again or find another way to contact them.

6

How can I go shopping on the internet?

Shopping on the internet, sometimes referred to as **e-commerce**, can be a blissful experience – sitting down with a drink to hand, you are a long way from the jostling crowds, the long queues, busy car parks and pickpockets. Come rain or shine, night or day, this virtual marketplace is open for business.

You might be feeling a little nervous about shopping on the internet, and this is very natural since you cannot see or feel the goods that you are buying or meet the shopkeepers face to face. But by being aware of possible hazards and areas where you need to tread carefully, shopping on the internet should be no more risky than buying by mail order or over the telephone.

Choosing where to shop

The internet gives you a shopping window onto a world of goods and services which aren't always readily available on the high street. But it's more important than ever to know who you are dealing with, because on the internet it is a lot easier for unscrupulous companies to conceal their identities.

Find your feet by exploring some of the websites of well-known retailers first. Take a guess at their web addresses based on their names, or type in their names into a search engine.

The web addresses of well-known retailers tend to be based on their company names. Some examples include:

argos.co.uk

boots.co.uk

debenhams.co.uk

iceland.co.uk

johnlewis.co.uk

lloydspharmacy.co.uk

marksandspencer.co.uk

sainsburys.co.uk

tesco.co.uk

whsmith.co.uk

Internet shopping checklist

✔ Make sure you know who the company or person is behind the website, and if in doubt, look up their telephone number and address and call them in person to double-check their details (be very wary of any site which does not give you full contact details).

✔ Check where the company is based. If it is outside the UK, you may want to avoid buying very expensive items from them, unless you know them well, to limit the risk of things going wrong or possible additional expenses, such as the cost of returning goods.

✔ A website that is up to date and professionally designed tends to fill you with more confidence about the retailer than a site which looks as if it has been put together in a teenager's bedroom. But fight the temptation to judge a company by the appearance of its website alone; an enticing website is no guarantee that it will deliver on its promises.

✔ If you haven't heard of a company, check whether the company is a registered member of a relevant trade association or subscribes to a code of good practice.

✔ Only buy from web retailers that enable you to send your credit card details via secure pages which encrypt the details as they are transmitted.

Coming up with the goods

Websites usually provide comprehensive information about products, including pictures, prices and descriptions. Some actually give you more detail than shops do; for example by including reviews and suggestions for other related items.

You will have to go through a selection process to find the things that you want to buy, down to details such as size and colour, depending on the type of product. Many sites provide a search facility which allows you to enter the product, brand name or service you are looking for. But if you are in the mood for browsing, then most sites will also provide you with a series of menus to help you get to what you want.

Most websites will give you a 'shopping basket' into which you place all the items that you have selected to buy and then invite you to the 'checkout', where the contents of your 'basket' are turned into an order (see Fig 11).

Fig 11 – To select items from the Tesco online superstore (*tesco.co.uk*), add them to your shopping basket, then proceed to the checkout to list everything you have picked

Reading the small print

As with all purchases, read the small print to make sure that there are no nasty surprises waiting for you. Look carefully at the price of what you are buying (especially if you have to convert from a price quoted in a different currency) and watch for additional, sometimes hidden, charges such as VAT, high delivery rates (particularly from overseas), packaging, taxes or duties and any extra charges for using a particular payment method.

Before you finally complete the order, read the Terms and Conditions on the retailer's website. Check the refund and return policies, what protections are offered in case things go wrong, how long delivery will take and, if the facility is offered on the site, the current stock level.

You should also read the retailer's privacy policy statement so that you understand what personal information they intend to collect and what they are going to do with it. There should always be the option to opt out of newsletters and other promotional mailings and any scheme which would pass on your personal information to third parties.

Making the payment

How often do you hand your credit card to a waiter in a restaurant or give out your account number over the telephone? These probably pose a greater security risk than giving out your credit card details online.

When you have checked your order and are ready to make the payment, check that the web page you are on is secure. Often a message will flash up on your screen to announce that you are entering a secure page; most importantly you should look out for a closed padlock symbol in the status bar at the bottom of your browser screen, and a web address beginning 'https', which both show that your details are protected when being sent (see Fig 12).

A web address beginning 'https' and a padlock symbol confirm that the web page is secure for entering payment information.

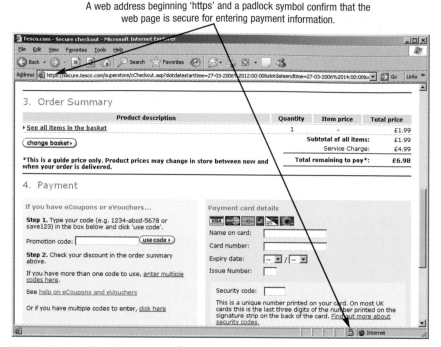

Fig 12 – You should only buy from retailers who offer secure pages. Look out for the padlock symbol and a web address beginning 'https'

As a last precaution, when you have finally placed your order, save copies of the information relating to the transaction. If you have a printer you can print this information out (select 'Print' from your browser), or save a copy of this web page to your computer by selecting the 'File' menu followed by 'Save As'.

Any good retailer will email you to acknowledge and summarise your order, giving you an order reference number to use in any further correspondence.

An example – amazon.co.uk

1. Find the right website

The most popular online purchases are CDs, DVDs and books. Many web retailers sell them, enabling customers to shop around for the cheapest prices and best service. One such retailer, *Amazon,* first traded in America with **amazon.com** They then expanded to Europe and established a UK site – **amazon.co.uk** This initially led to many confused UK shoppers buying from the American site by mistake, adding the cost of overseas postage to their orders.

Therefore, if you are browsing for something to buy on a site which is not specifically aimed at the UK market, look out for a signpost to a UK-only site, or enquire if there is one.

2. Find the right item

You will need to go through a process of searching the site to find the item(s) that you want. *Amazon* provides a useful search box which, for a book, allows you to specify the title, author or subject (see Fig 13).

Enter a description of the item into the search box

Fig 13 – Search the site to find the items you want

3. Inspect the item

Once you have found an item, find out more about it by reading the description of it, or zoom in to inspect a more descriptive photograph of it (see Fig 14). At this stage you should also look into the full price of the item, details of the retailer's refund and return policies and, where possible, product reviews, an idea of current stock levels and how long it will take to deliver the item to your door.

Look at details such as the description, price, availability, reviews etc, to help you decide

If you're satisfied, add it to your shopping basket

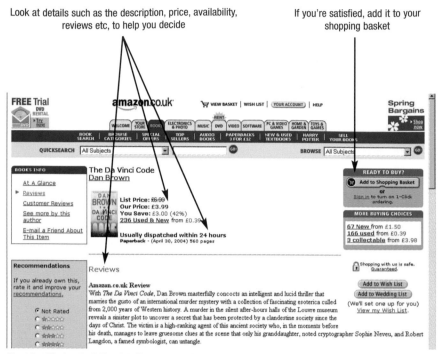

Fig 14 – Find out all the details you can about the items you want

4. You've found the item, now you're ready to buy

The website should give you the opportunity to inspect the items in your shopping basket at any time, update any of them or take any out that you have since changed your mind about. When you are satisfied that you have everything you want, you then proceed to the checkout (see Fig 15).

5. Time to pay

When you are ready to pay, you will be asked to select a payment method and provide your credit/debit card number, expiry date and, for some cards, the issue number and start date. Remember to look out for signs that the current web page is secure. **You should not give out your credit card details unless the page is secure** (as shown in Fig 16).

Fig 15 – Confirm when you are happy with the items in your shopping basket and want to finish shopping

Remember to look out for signs that
the current page is secure

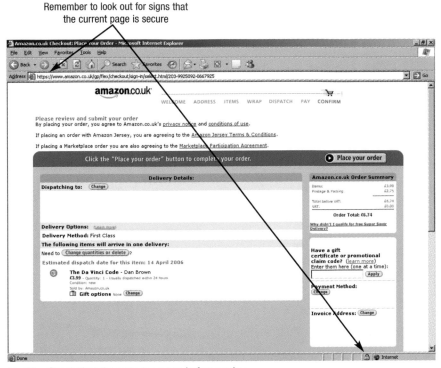

Fig 16 – Check that the page is secure before paying

You will also need to give your name, email address and delivery address.
You may also be invited to register, which is usually to save you having to
retype your details if you visit the site again – but some retailers also provide
a facility to enable you to track the progress of your order online.

6. Confirmation of order

At the end of the process you will be asked to confirm the details you have
given, and then the sale is complete. Any good retailer will also confirm your
order by email with a reference number.

Other ways to shop

An extremely popular way of looking for a bargain on anything, from the
weird and wonderful to the plain and practical, is to use an internet auction
site like eBay (**ebay.co.uk**). eBay's home page provides a list of main
categories (such as clothes, crafts, music), which continually subdivide so
that you can get a very close description to a particular item you are looking

for; or you can simply type in the item as a search term. You can choose how to sort the items – whether by price or in the order in which the auction closes. Often photographs accompany a short description of the item, and the cost of postage that the buyer pays is clearly listed.

If you find an item you want to buy, you decide on the price you'd like to pay and place a bid. If at the end of the auction your bid is the highest, then the purchase goes through. The most common way to pay for items on eBay is using their secure payment system called Paypal which transfers money from the buyer's bank account or credit card to the seller. The site provides worked examples and helpful guidelines for first-time users, which are worth looking at before you launch into your first auction.

Another way of shopping when you know the item you want to buy but not necessarily where to get it or how much it is likely to cost, is to try a shopping search engine like **kelkoo.co.uk** (see Fig 17) or **froogle.co.uk** These websites let you compare the features and price of products across a range of retailers and buy the one that meets your needs, if you want to, without you having to wade through lots of individual websites.

Fig 17 – Compare products, such as digital radios in this example, across different retailers with shopping search engines like *kelkoo.co.uk*

7

How can I manage my money online?

More and more of us are choosing to manage our personal finances using the internet. It's quick, convenient, available all the time from anywhere, and as safe as any other way of handling money.

Online banking

It's very likely that your existing bank or building society will offer online banking, allowing you to remain loyal to your current provider, while taking advantage of the convenience of being able to perform all routine transactions – such as viewing your balance, paying bills, transferring money between a savings and current account, and ordering a cheque book – anytime, day or night, from any computer connected to the internet.

If you rarely visit your bank or building society, then why accept the low interest rates and high fees some of them charge for services you are not using? You could switch to an online-only bank that offers competitive rates but does not have any 'high-street' presence. The main disadvantages to consider are that deposits by cheque will have to be sent by post, customer service is either online or by phone, and you may only be able to issue a limited number of cheques.

Banks and building societies offering online banking usually have demonstrations on their websites, which provide a simple way of seeing what it's like without committing yourself (see Fig 18). If you do want a little longer to make up your mind whether it is for you, consider opening an internet account with a small amount of money and testing some of its features for a while.

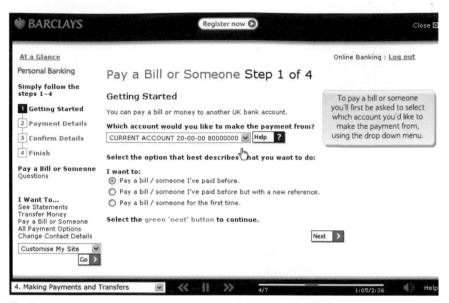

Fig 18 – Pay someone from an online bank account, for example using *barclays.co.uk*

If you do decide to take the plunge and start banking online, then you will need to complete an application form. You can usually do this online at the bank/building society's website, and you will then be sent a passcode in the post. To open up your internet bank account, you type in some of the details you provided at registration together with the passcode.

As with shopping online, it is wise to be aware of the possibility of fraud and scams, so here are a few tips to help stay safe:

* Keep your personal details secret. Never write down your passcode or other security information unless they are well disguised and don't reveal them to another person. Also, destroy the passcode notice you get through the post as soon as you receive it.
* Always log out. When you have finished, select the button on your banking website labelled 'log out', and never leave your computer unattended whilst you are logged in if there is any risk of someone you cannot trust looking at your details.
* Never reveal your personal details by email. Increasingly, criminals are sending emails which purport to be from banks or building societies – they ask for personal details to be updated or confirmed, and link to very credible imitations of the real banking websites. Remember that your bank or building society will never ask for your personal details in this way.

* Ensure that there is a closed padlock symbol in the status bar at the bottom of your browser screen before accessing the banking website, and that the web address has changed from 'http' to 'https' to indicate a secure connection.

* Ensure that you use a firewall and anti-virus software (see Chapter 3).

Benefits and taxes

It is possible to check your eligibility for a wide range of state benefits (such as Housing Benefit, Council Tax Benefit, Carers Allowance, Disability Living Allowance, Attendance Allowance, Incapacity Benefit) and make applications online. The Directgov website (**direct.gov.uk** – see Fig 19) aims to bring together a lot of government services and information in this one website, and the website of The Pension Service (**thepensionservice.gov.uk**) provides useful tools such as a calculator to help estimate how much Pension Credit you may be entitled to.

Fig 19 – *Direct.gov.uk* provides a wide range of government information and services online

If you have to complete tax returns, then you can save yourself the effort of calculating the tax, and have instant access to your statement and make payments by completing the self assessment online (**hmrc.gov.uk**).

What else?

Although it is no substitute for independent financial advice, the web does provide easy access to reviews, league tables and customer comments to help compare different financial products and inform your decisions about saving and investment options (see for example **fsa.gov.uk/consumer** or **fool.co.uk**).

As well as helping you plan the best way to save or invest your pounds, the web is a useful tool to help you save your pennies as well. Consumer websites such as **uswitch.com** and **moneysupermarket.com** compare the latest rates offered by energy suppliers, insurers, and credit card companies, which might help you reduce your household expenditure bills.

If you are planning a trip abroad, you can track the exchange rate of the currency of your destination using one of the many financial and travel websites (for example **bankofscotland.co.uk** or **thomascook.co.uk**). Biding your time in this way might earn you extra pounds' worth of currency.

8

How can I chat to people on the internet?

A problem shared is a problem halved, particularly if you can find half a dozen other people to share it with. So whether you simply want to track down someone who can help you answer a question that has been plaguing you for days, or you are embarking on a new venture and could do with some handy hints from people who have relevant experience, or you have a passion for a new book or hobby that you are eager to share, the internet provides access to worldwide communities of people who share your interests, have been through similar experiences, or have interesting tales to tell.

Message boards

One of the easiest ways to share your views on a subject is by using a message board. Message boards (also called 'bulletin boards') are typically pages in websites which invite you to post up a message or question that other people can see and reply to. They are a useful way of sharing experiences and tips with wide groups of people.

Messages are presented in a list, known as a 'thread', which shows the original message, the responses to the message and the responses to the responses, so you can follow an entire conversation or just the sections you are interested in.

Some message boards are moderated by a person who decides which messages to allow or to remove, but most are unmoderated, so people are free to add just about anything they like.

As with other spaces where people spend time, there are rules of polite behaviour when using message boards which you are expected to observe. Before you participate, you should spend a little time learning the purpose and the 'rules' of the message board before posting any messages of your own. They can be quite intimidating to the first-time user.

The BBC website includes message boards for some of its popular programmes, such as *Gardeners' World* (**bbc.co.uk/gardening** – see Fig 20) in which, for example, you might see messages from people sharing tips on tackling garden pests.

Fig 20 – The BBC's gardening message boards (*bbc.co.uk/gardening*) are popular and easy to use

Mailing lists

You sign up to join a mailing list (also known as an 'email group') simply by supplying an email address and a password. The idea is that anyone who has subscribed to that list/group can send a message which is then sent out to everyone else on the list by email. Messages are normally also published to a message board on a web page. In turn anyone in the list can comment on the message, replying by email or by visiting the web page.

Sometimes it is also possible to opt to receive updates as a 'digest', which saves you being overwhelmed with a daily flood of emails; you simply receive a periodic summary of the messages. You may also find it helpful to create a new folder into which you can save any of these messages that you wish to keep for future reference. (To create a new folder, select the 'File' menu, followed by 'Folder', followed by 'New' and type in a name for the new folder.)

If you go away on holiday, it might be a good idea to temporarily unsubscribe, just as you would temporarily stop your newspaper delivery, because a list which is particularly popular will generate many messages a day which could overload your mailbox.

Websites such as **http://uk.groups.yahoo.com** (see Fig 21) provide email groups that you can join. If you don't find any that match your interests, they also provide a simple way to set up your own.

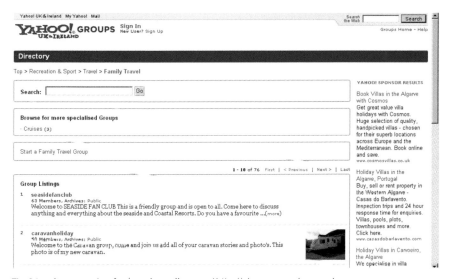

Fig 21 – An example of a travel email group (*http://uk.groups.yahoo.com*)

Chat sites

Unlike message boards and mailing lists, chat sites offer a way to hold conversations in 'real time', in a similar way to having a telephone conversation with a number of people at the same time, except that you type instead of talk.

You need to register to become a member of a chat site and to think of a nickname, which will be the name by which people will know you and address you inside the chat site. Some chat sites invite you to provide a little bit of information about yourself. This is useful if you are keen to meet people with a similar interest, or you want to promote a society or club that you belong to. However, remember that things may not always be as they seem – it is very easy to pretend to be someone else on the internet, so be cautious about giving out too much personal information.

The number of chat sites is growing all the time, so it shouldn't be too difficult to find one that you feel comfortable with and covers topics that interest you. Try typing in a set of search words (such as 'dieting chat') into a search engine to find a chat site which covers a topic that you are interested in.

Instant messaging

Just like chat sites, 'instant messaging' provides a way to hold conversations with other people over the internet. The main difference is that everyone taking part must have the same, or compatible, instant messaging software. You then choose who you want to involve in your conversation and you can add voice and live video if you have a web camera. The software is free and very simple to download – examples are *AOL Messenger* (**aol.co.uk/aim**) and *Yahoo Messenger* (**http://uk.messenger.yahoo.com**).

When you download the software, you choose a nickname (sometimes referred to as your 'screen name' or 'ID'). The friends or relatives you want to chat to also download the software to their computers and choose their IDs. You can add IDs to the list of people you would like to chat to, just like an address book.

You can use the messenger software to check whether someone is online by selecting their ID, and if they are online, send an invitation to them to start chatting.

9

How can the internet help me research my family history?

Researching family history is one of the most popular internet hobbies. Thousands and thousands more people every year are finding that the internet can help them in their quest to discover more about their roots.

The first step in researching your family history is to gather as many old photographs, documents and details of names, dates, places, and key family events from relatives and friends as you can. With these as your starting points, you have the pick of a huge range of websites to help you dig deeper into your family's past.

Tracing records

A website called 'FreeBMD' (which stands for Free Births, Marriages and Deaths) at **freebmd.org.uk** provides internet access to millions of UK birth, marriage and death records covering the period 1837–1983. You can apply online at the website of the General Register Office for England and Wales at **gro.gov.uk** for a hard copy of a birth, marriage or death certificate. The Register Offices for Scotland and Northern Ireland also have equivalent websites.

Parish registers are useful for tracing baptisms, marriages and burials, especially those that date before the introduction of civil registration. The website 'FreeREG' at **freereg.org.uk** provides free searches.

The internet can also be used to study military records. The Commonwealth War Graves Commission website at **cwgc.org** provides personal details (such as the name of the spouse and parents), service details and places of commemoration for those who died whilst serving with Commonwealth forces during the First and Second World Wars. Websites like **forcesreunited.org.uk** and **comradesandcolleagues.com** can also be valuable in helping trace old friends of people who used to, or currently, serve with the forces. The BBC's family history website provides a list of links to websites containing useful records and resources for anyone tracing ancestors in the forces at **bbc.co.uk/familyhistory/bloodlines/military.shtml**

Another line of useful research might be immigration and emigration records. The internet can help here as well by providing direct access to the national archives of many countries, ship passenger lists and even transportation registers if your ancestor happened to have fallen foul of the law at that time and been sentenced to transportation. The BBC's family history website provides a list of links to websites containing useful records and resources for anyone tracing ancestors who migrated to or from the UK at **bbc.co.uk/familyhistory/bloodlines/migration.shtml**

Searching the censuses

The census records are extremely useful to family history researchers because they document the names and occupations of household occupants, and exact ages and birthplaces in later records. The National Archives website (**nationalarchives.gov.uk/census**) provides a set of useful links to help you quickly search the 1851–1901 censuses for England and Wales online for free (see Fig 22). There is a small fee to pay for accessing more detailed information or downloading digital images of original census pages. 'Scotland's People' at **scotlandspeople.gov.uk** is also a pay-per-view website and census information is available on the website of the Public Record Office of Northern Ireland (at **proni.gov.uk**).

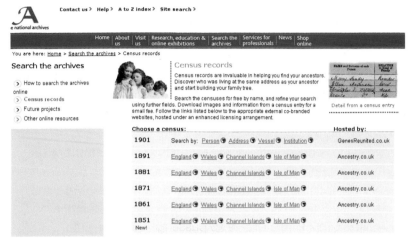

Fig 22 – The National Archives website (*nationalarchives.gov.uk/census*) provides quick links to the 1851–1901 censuses for England and Wales

Researching local archives

Many local authority websites contain information about record offices as well as local history clubs and classes, local studies libraries and archive services. Alternatively, save some leg-work by using a directory such as **nationalarchives.gov.uk/archon** or **familia.org.uk** to find out what family history research services and archive record repositories are available in your geographical area of interest.

Other family history research tools on the internet

1. Search engines
Search engines should not be ignored as tools which can help you trace your family history. Many people get started by simply typing their surname into a search engine.

2. Contact other family history researchers
Type in the search words 'family history chat' into a search engine and you will see that there is no shortage of chat sites, mailing lists and message boards through which you can share tips and advice with like-minded family history researchers.

One such website is called 'Rootsweb' (at **rootsweb.com**). It provides thousands of mailing lists and message boards, enabling many ways to search, including by name, topic or the geographical area you are interested in.

3. Contact your local family history society

The website of the Federation of Family History Societies at **ffhs.org.uk** provides the contact details (including email address and web address, if available) of local societies, which often hold lectures, organise visits and provide advice. Societies in Scotland are listed on the website of the Scottish Association of Family History Societies (at **safhs.org.uk**).

4. Research old maps

A website called 'Old Maps' at **old-maps.co.uk** provides access to digital historical maps using part of an address, an Ordnance Survey grid reference or a place name.

5. Find a family tree software program

There are many software programs on the market to help you systematically organise the information you collect about your ancestors. Many of them advertise on the web or provide free downloads, and you can also compare reviews or get recommendations from current users via message boards.

10

Where can I find out more about the internet?

Just as you need to jump into the driving seat of a car to learn about driving, so you need to take the plunge and start 'surfing' to learn more about the internet. Follow some of the processes described in this book, and then experiment for yourself.

The internet is also a resource in itself. You will find many websites, including message boards, providing tips and practical advice for internet newcomers. Here are a few ideas for some places to start.

Internet resources

bbc.co.uk/webwise
This website is a very useful resource, catering for all levels of internet experience. The site includes a step-by-step tutorial, access to instant answers to your questions and articles about topical internet issues.

ageconcern.org.uk/discuss
The Age Concern website includes a discussion board for sharing questions, comments, tips and ideas to help you make the most of the internet (see Fig 23).

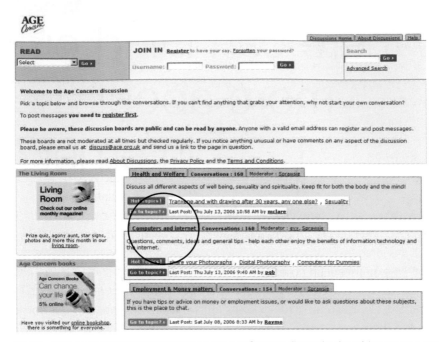

Fig 23 – Talk to other internet beginners on the Age Concern discussion board (*ageconcern.org.uk/discuss*)

Search engines

Try a search engine such as Google (**google.co.uk**) or Yahoo!
(**yahoo.co.uk**) and type in a search phrase like 'Internet Beginners Guides'
for links to articles, guides and internet dictionaries.

Courses

There are also courses available which will help you build confidence and
practical experience of the internet.

Age Concern

Age Concern offers computer taster sessions across the UK, giving people
the chance to use the internet and learn other computer skills in friendly and
informal environments with other beginners. To find out if there is an Age
Concern taster session in your area, email **diginetwork@ace.org.uk** or
phone 020 8765 7231.

UK online centres

UK online centres aim to help people who are new to computers and the internet. Some will even have staff or volunteers on hand. Your nearest centre could be in your local school, your public library, a church or community centre or the offices of a local company. To find out where your nearest centre is, phone 0800 77 1234.

Learndirect

Learndirect is a government-backed service which provides access to courses available via the internet or in one of the national network of Learndirect centres. Course details can be found on its website at **learndirect.co.uk** or by phoning its information line on 0800 101 901.

Many further education colleges also run internet beginners' classes as well as more advanced courses on subjects such as how to design your own website.

Other resources

Magazines such as *ComputerActive* are available in newsagents and bookshops or by subscription, and are written in plain English for readers who are new to computers as well as the internet.

Last but not least, talking to people around you – friends and family – will give you a valuable insight into things that have worked well, or not so well for them, providing a wonderful pool of experience and ideas to dip into.

Glossary

ADSL (Asymmetric Digital Subscriber Line)   More commonly known as *broadband,* ADSL uses a standard telephone line to transfer data at high speed. The term 'asymmetric' refers to the fact that data moves faster from the telephone exchange to a home computer than in the other direction. This makes it particularly suitable for internet use, where more information is received than is sent. An ADSL *modem* enables a computer to send/receive data via broadband.

Bandwidth   The amount of information that you can send/receive using your internet connection, measured in bits per second (bps), kilobits per second (Kbps), or megabits per second (Mbps).

Broadband   High-speed internet access with a permanent connection to the internet, known as 'always on', permitting unlimited use for a fixed monthly charge.

Bulletin board   (see *Message board*)

Cache   *Web browsers* hold copies of recently visited web pages in a directory on your hard disk. This disk memory space is called the cache. When you return to a page you've recently looked at, the browser can get it from the cache rather than the original server, saving you time. The disadvantage is that it will sometimes show you an old version of a page from your disk when a newer one is available on the web but you can check for a newer version by using the Refresh or Reload option in your browser.

Chat site   A special kind of *website* which enables conversation between people visiting the website at the same time. Chat sites are popular as meeting places for people who may never actually meet each other in person, but who can chat to each other like old friends by typing, reading and responding to text messages.

Dial-up   Creating a temporary connection to the internet using a *modem* over an ordinary voice telephone line.

Downloading   This is the process of transferring files from a computer on the internet to your own computer through your connection (such as down a telephone line) – for example when you receive an *email* or view a *website*.

E-commerce   The process of buying and selling over the internet.

Email   Short for 'electronic mail'. It is the internet version of the postal service. Instead of putting a letter into a postbox, you send a message from your computer through your connection (such as down a telephone line) to another person who also has access to email.

Email address   To exchange email messages with friends, family and other contacts, and to register for many type of internet services, you need your own email address, which will typically look something like this: heatherbloggs@hotmail.com

Firewall   *Software, hardware,* or a combination of both, that provides protection from intruders or hackers who might try to use the internet to break into your computer.

Hard disk   The disk inside your computer where your programs are stored. Disk capacity is measured in megabytes (MB), or gigabytes (GB) which are approximately one thousand times larger than megabytes.

Hardware   Physical computer equipment, such as keyboards, printers and modems.

Hyperlink   A hyperlink may be a word or a graphic. When it is clicked with a mouse, a new web page, or part of the same page, opens automatically in your *web browser*. When a hyperlink is text, it typically displays in a different colour and may also be underlined. A text hyperlink that has already been visited is usually displayed in a different colour.

Internet   A worldwide collection of computers joined by networks which are linked to each other via communication links such as telephone lines. To join the internet all you have to do is connect your computer to this network.

Internet Service Provider (ISP)   A company which provides you with access to the internet from your computer.

Mailing list   A service that collects messages and broadcasts them to a specific group of people by email, enabling a discussion to take place. Mailing lists usually serve a particular interest group.

Mail server   A computer managed by your *ISP* which gives access to email messages.

Message board   A page in a *website* which is used to display a topic or a question to which anyone can respond, and these responses are then displayed for all to read and respond to.

Modem   A device which converts the digital data from your computer into sound signals which are transmitted over a standard telephone line, and converts sound signals back again into digital data which can be understood by your computer.

Network   Computers which are joined together by cables and software are called networks. They can swap information and messages between themselves.

Offline   This means working on a computer that does *not* currently have a 'live' connection to the internet.

Online   This means working on a computer that *does* currently have a 'live' connection to the internet.

Operating system   This is software that manages the hardware and software on a computer. The operating system performs tasks such as controlling and allocating memory, prioritising the processing of instructions, and managing files.

POP3 (Post Office Protocol 3)   This is a standard for receiving *email*. It is built into the most popular email programs and *web browsers*.

Processor   The 'brains' of your computer. The faster the processor's speed – measured in megahertz (MHz) or gigahertz (GHz) – the more calculations and data the computer can process.

RAM (Random Access Memory)   The memory your computer uses to open and run all the different programs, measured in megabytes (MB).

Router   A **hardware** device that forwards data between computers.

Search engine/directory   A special kind of **website** which allows you to enter words or select from list of subjects and categories to search for a topic. A search engine combs the web for pages relevant to your search. A web directory uses real people to add new web pages to their lists.

Software   Also called computer programs or applications. Instructs your computer to carry out the tasks involved in browsing the web, handling emails, and word processing for example.

Uploading   This is the process of transferring files from your own computer to a computer on the internet through your connection (such as down a telephone line) – for example when you send an **email** or publish a web page you have created at home to a live **website**.

URL (Uniform Resource Locator)   (see **web address**)

USB port   A type of socket found on the front or back of your computer that enables it to share data quickly with **hardware** devices.

Viruses   Dangerous computer programs that are able to modify other programs.

Web   Provides a way of viewing the information stored on computers connected to the internet.

Web address   Identifies the location on the internet of a website or page. Typically looks something like this : **http://www.ageconcern.org.uk**

Web browser   A type of **software** that enables your computer to load and display pages in a website. The most popular web browser is Microsoft's *Internet Explorer.*

Website   A collection of pages which can consist of text, pictures, moving images and sound which together describe an organisation/product/service, etc.

Webmail   Short for 'web-based email'. A website (such as **hotmail.com**) that provides the facility to send and receive emails from any computer connected to the internet.

World wide web (www)   (see *web*)

Index

Age Concern Books

Age Concern publishes a wide range of valuable handbooks that provide practical, expert advice on a number of issues. Among other things, our books help thousands of people claim the benefits they are entitled to, make sense of pensions, cut down on tax payments, and plan for their retirement. They offer user-friendly guidance on computing and surfing the net, as well as dealing with health issues. There's also a comprehensive range of books for carers and care professionals. To find out more visit our website or phone our hotline now and order a FREE catalogue.

To order a book:

- Visit our website: **www.ageconcern.org.uk/bookshop** (secure online bookshop)

- Telephone our hotline: **0870 44 22 120**
  (Opening hours: 9am-7pm Mon to Fri, 9am-5pm Sat and Sun)

- Send a cheque or money order to:
  Age Concern Books, Units 5 and 6 Industrial Estate, Brecon, Powys LD3 8LA. Cheques payable to Age Concern England for the appropriate amount plus p&p.

Postage and packing: mainland UK and Northern Ireland: £1.99 for the first book, 75p for each additional book up to a maximum of £7.50. For customers ordering from outside the mainland UK and NI: credit card payment only; please telephone for international postage rates or email sales@ageconcernbooks.co.uk.

Bulk order discounts are available on orders of 50 or more copies of the same title. For details, please contact Age Concern Books on 0870 44 22 120.

Age Concern Factsheets

Age Concern produces comprehensive factsheets designed to answer many of the questions older people (or those advising them) may have. These include money and benefits, health, community care, leisure and education, and housing. For free factsheets telephone the information line on 0800 00 99 66 (8am-7pm, seven days a week, every week of the year). Alternatively you may prefer to download them free from our website: www.ageconcern.org.uk

Everyday computer activities
A step by step guide for older home users
By Jackie Sherman

Many people own a computer but don't know how to use all the functions on it. Perhaps you are in this position. You may not be aware of the huge range of things you can do on your computer or where to get help. This book will take you step-by-step through many exciting and useful activities including:

- digital cameras
- scanning pictures
- playing games
- shopping on the internet
- creating greetings cards
- making labels and much more

All information is well supported with colour illustrations and screenshots.
£7.99 + p&p ISBN 0-86242-403-8

Getting the most from your computer
A practical guide for older home users
By Jackie Sherman

This bestselling guide offers essential information, help and guidance, for anyone keen to learn more about their personal computers.

Topics include:
- buying and setting up a new system
- an introduction to all the most commonly-used packages such as Word, Excel and PowerPoint
- help and guidance on using the internet and email

With step-by-step instructions, exercises at the end of each chapter and screen shots and illustrations throughout, it is the perfect guide to have handy when you are exploring the wide range of applications available to you.
£7.99 + p&p ISBN 0-86242-392-9

Your Rights: working over 50
A guide to your employment options
By Andrew Harrop and Susie Munro

As most of us need to earn a living, which means we spend a great deal of our time at work. It is almost inevitable that there will be challenges and difficulties during our career. This book is essential reading for anyone over 50 in work, leaving work, or looking for work.

It includes information on a wide range of topics; from age discrimination and redundancy to retirement planning; from self employment to job hunting. Whether you need to update your skills or manage a dispute with your employer, you'll find the best advice right here.

£8.99 + p&p ISBN 0862424259

Your Rights 2006/07
A guide to money benefits for older people
By Sally West

Your Rights has established itself as *the* money benefits guide for older people. Updated annually, and written in clear, jargon-free language, it ensures that older people – and their advisers – can easily understand the complexities of state benefits and discover the full range of financial support available to them.

£5.99 + p&p ISBN 0-86242-415-1

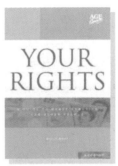

Your Rights to health care
Helping older people get the best from the NHS
By Lorna Easterbrook

Many people are unsure what NHS services they are entitled to. Help is at hand with this comprehensive guide written specifically for the over 60s. It covers many areas, including opticians, dentists, GPs, hospitals, and support for long-term illness. It also guides you through all you need to know to make a complaint and your rights to alternative therapies and private healthcare.

Contents include:
- eyesight and hearing services
- mental health
- going into and coming out of hospital
- NHS care where you live
- organ and blood donation
- making complaints

£7.99 + p&p ISBN 0-86242-398-8

Understanding taxes and savings 2006/07
Make more of your money
By Paul Lewis

Many millions of pounds are lost each year through bad savings and inaccurate tax payments. Some people don't know this is happening, while others aren't sure how to put things right. Paul Lewis, the acclaimed broadcaster and journalist, is here to help. In this user-friendly handbook he shows you how to avoid paying too much tax, while saving money for retirement.
£7.99 + p&p ISBN 0-86242-417-8

Your guide to pensions 2006/07
Planning ahead to boost retirement income
By Sue Ward

For many people of working age, planning for retirement is an increasingly important issue. If you're one of the growing numbers of people who are keen to improve their income in later life, you couldn't do better than turn to Sue Ward's simple and practical handbook for help. Updated annually, it explains all major types of pension schemes as well as other forms of retirement income.
£7.99 + p&p ISBN 0-86242-418-6

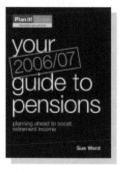

Using your home as capital 2006/7
A guide to raising money from the value of your home

Many older people find themselves short of money, yet they live in their own, often valuable, properties. Through a wide variety of schemes, people aged 55 and over can now use the value of their homes to obtain a lump sum of capital or a regular additional income without having to move home. This book is an essential guide to the benefits and the problems which can arise in a constantly changing and rapidly developing market.
£6.99 + p&p ISBN 0-86242-419-4

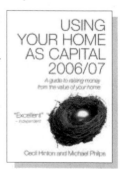

All finance titles updated annually.
For details of the current edition, please telephone 0870 44 22 120
or look on our website: www.ageconcern.org.uk/bookshop

Choices in retirement
Your guide to the essentials
By Ro Lyon

This bestselling book, now in its fourth edition, is designed to encourage everyone to view retirement as an opportunity to be embraced. Positive and upbeat, it aims to provide people who are about to retire – or have just retired – with suggestions and practical information that will be useful for the years ahead. It includes several new sections on using the NHS, utilities, adjusting to being at home, and grandparenting. Other topics include:

- Managing your money
- Staying healthy and keeping active
- Transport and moving home

£9.99 + p&p ISBN 0-86242-412-7

Choices in retirement housing
Your guide to all the options
EAC, ARHM and AIMS

As people grow older, their housing needs often change. This book guides readers through all the areas to be explored, and answers the many questions that are often raised. Complete with case studies and useful contacts it provides all the vital information needed to make an informed decision. Contents include:

- Making life easier if staying in your own home.
- The benefits – and possible downside – of retirement housing, plus what is available.
- Living in retirement housing – what it's like, scheme manager's role, legal rights.
- Renting and leasehold retirement housing.
- Legal aspects – how to complain, your rights, lease 'jargon buster'.

The book covers England only.
£9.99 + p&p ISBN 0-86242-413-5

Retiring to Spain
Everything you need to know
By Cyril Holbrook

Once free of the shackles of earning a living, thousands of people make the momentous move to head south to the sun. Living abroad is an entirely different experience from going there on holiday. This book will help people avoid many of the pitfalls, and enable them to make the transition to a sunny and healthy retirement. It contains chapters on:

- Pros and cons of living abroad, where to settle
- Finances and property, town halls and taxes
- Healthcare
- Common complaints, going home
- Useful addresses

£7.99 + p&p ISBN 0-86242-385-6

Taking control: bladder and bowel problems

By Kerry Lee

Bladder and bowel problems can affect both men and women, of all ages, and can lead to feelings of anxiety, embarrassment and despair. This excellent guide, complete with relevant case studies, breaks the taboo subject of such problems and provides answers to questions that will enable readers to feel more in control of their problem.

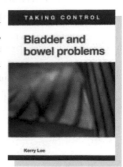

Chapters include:
- Causes of bladder and bowel problems
- Help available
- Dealing with related issues
- Bladder and bowel problems

£6.99 + p&p ISBN 0-86242-386-4

Taking control of your pain

By Toni Battison

One in seven people in the UK suffer from chronic pain. Whilst much progress has been made in recent years towards understanding and managing pain, it can still pose a major problem. This book gives essential guidance on how to control pain effectively. It is full of practical information and support, as well as signposting readers to other relevant sources of help and advice.

Chapters include:
- Pain – physical and psychological effects
- Pain – types and common causes
- Diagnosis and assessment
- Dealing with pain – orthodox and self-help treatments
- Stress relief and non-orthodox treatments
- Looking at your lifestyle

£6.99 + p&p ISBN 0-86242-387-2

Intimate relations
Living and loving in later life

By Doctor Sarah Brewer

Sexual problems in later life often remain a taboo subject, but this book addresses them with a frankness readers will appreciate. Age-related health problems need not get in the way of a fulfilling relationship. Even for people who are less physically active or mobile than they used to be, there are many ways of sharing a fulfilling and enjoyable love life.

Chapters include:
- Changing body, changing needs
- Low sex drive
- Being alone
- Seeking help
- Female and male sex problems

£9.99 + p&p ISBN 0-86242-384-8

The Carers Handbook Series

Essential reading for all those caring for a relative or friend

- They are packed full of information, practical checklists and case studies
- They are examine all the options available and point carers towards specialist help
- They are are up to date on recent guidelines and issues

Caring for someone with an alcohol problem
Mike Ward £6.99 + p&p ISBN 0-86242-372-4

Caring for someone with arthritis
Jim Pollard £6.99 + p&p ISBN 0-86242-373-2

Caring for someone with cancer
Toni Battison £6.99 + p&p ISBN 0-86242-382-1

Caring for someone with dementia
Jane Brotchie £6.99 + p&p ISBN 0-86242-368-6

Caring for someone with depression
Toni Battison £6.99 + p&p ISBN 0-86242-389-9

Caring for someone with diabetes
Marina Lewycka £6.99 + p&p ISBN 0-86242-374-0

Caring for someone who is dying
Penny Mares £6.99 + p&p ISBN 0-86242-370-8

Caring for someone with a hearing loss
Marina Lewycka £6.99 + p&p ISBN 0-86242-380-5

Caring for someone with a heart problem
Toni Battison £6.99 + p&p ISBN 0-86242-371-6

Caring for someone with memory loss
Toni Battison £6.99 + p&p ISBN 0-86242-358-9

Caring for someone with a sight problem
Marina Lewycka £6.99 + p&p ISBN 0-86242-381-3

Caring for someone who has had a stroke
Philip Coyne with Penny Mares £6.99 + p&p ISBN 0-86242-36

Carer's Handbook: What to do and who to turn to
Marina Lewycka £6.99 + p&p ISBN 0-86242-366-X

Caring for someone in their own home
Helen Howard £9.99 + p&p ISBN 0-86242-362-7

Caring for someone at a distance
Julie Spencer-Cingöz £6.99 + p&p ISBN 0-86242-367-8

Choices for the carer of an elderly relative
Marina Lewycka £6.99 + p&p ISBN 0-86242-375-9

Notes

Notes

Notes